WITHDRAWN

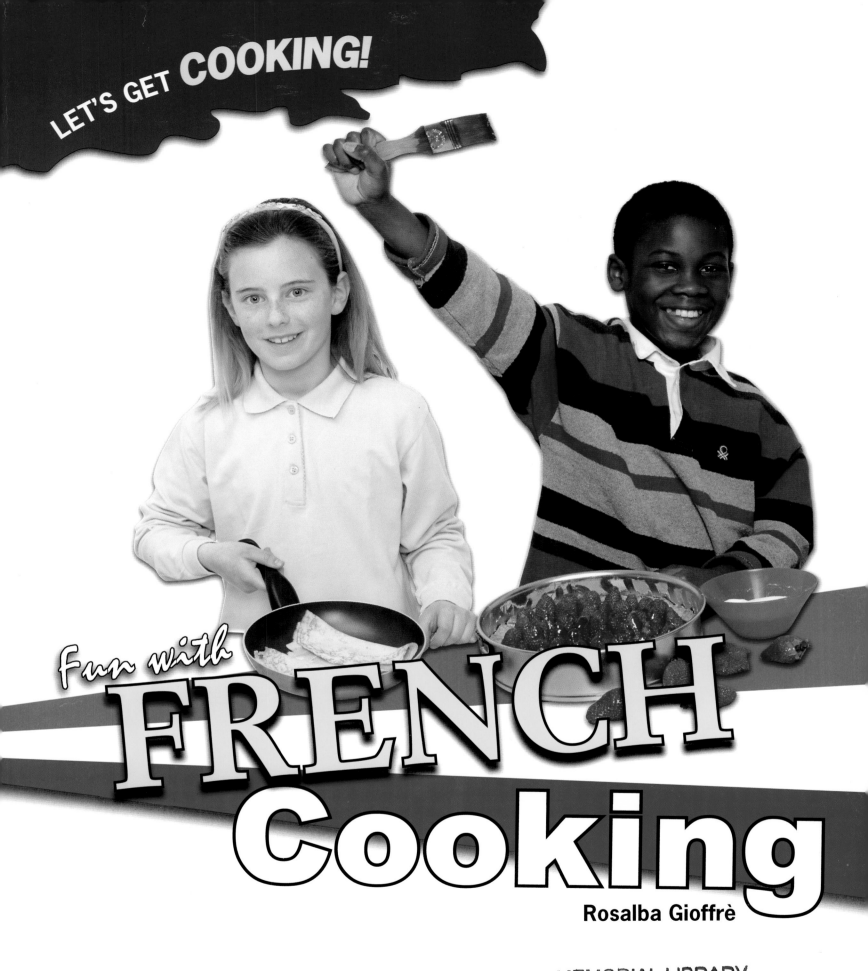

LET'S GET COOKING!

Fun with FRENCH Cooking

Rosalba Gioffrè

PowerKiDS press

New York

MEMORIAL LIBRARY
500 N. DUNTON
ARLINGTON HEIGHTS, IL 60004

Published in 2010 by The Rosen Publishing Group, Inc.
29 East 21st Street, New York, NY 10010

Copyright © 2010 McRae Books Srl

All rights reserved. No part of this book may be reproduced in any form without permission in writing from the publisher, except by a reviewer.

U.S. Editor: Kara Murray

Photo Credits: All images by Marco Lanza and Walter Mericchi.

Library of Congress Cataloging-in-Publication Data

Gioffrè, Rosalba.
  Fun with French cooking / Rosalba Gioffrè.
    p. cm. — (Let's get cooking!)
  Includes index.
  ISBN 978-1-4358-3454-5 (library binding) — ISBN 978-1-4358-3473-6 (pbk.) — ISBN 978-1-4358-3474-3 (6-pack)
  1. Cookery, French—Juvenile literature. I. Title.
  TX719.G558 2010
  641.5941—dc22

                          2009008649

Printed in China

Contents

Introduction

French food is so good that it has become famous all over the world. Many people think of it as a **cuisine** that is hard to cook, but there are many dishes that young chefs can prepare successfully. In this book, there are 14 recipes with step-by-step photographs. Follow the instructions carefully and you will be able to serve delicious meals for your friends and family. Each recipe has special tips and tricks to help you get it right from the start. Pages 18–19 focus on the Feast of the Kings, a festival that children in France celebrate on January 6. So, dig in, or as the French say, *Bon appétit!*

> **!** When cooking, you should always have an adult with you in the kitchen to help. Many of the tools used to prepare these recipes and others can be dangerous. Always be very careful when using a knife or a stove.

Croque-Monsieur

(KROHK-mis-YUR)

This toasted sandwich was invented in a bar in Paris in 1910. Not only is it tasty, it is also very easy to make. It's a sort of French fast food, and you can experiment with different variations. For example, try topping it with a fried egg. This is called a *croque-madame*!

1 Let the butter soften at room temperature. It should be soft but not melted. Use a knife to spread it onto one side of the bread.

2 If you are not using sliced cheese, grate the cheese. Make sure you keep your fingertips away from the grater.

TIPS & TRICKS

Ask an adult to help you when putting the croque-monsieur into or taking it out of the oven. If you do it yourself, wear thick oven mitts to protect your hands.

Ingredients

1 tablespoon (16 g) butter

2 slices bread

1 ounce (30 g) Gruyère or Swiss cheese

2 slices ham

3 Cover one of the slices of bread with the ham. **Trim** off any extra ham and place it in the middle. **Sprinkle** the grated cheese or lay the sliced cheese over the ham.

Place most of the cheese in the center of the sandwich to keep it from oozing out.

Utensils

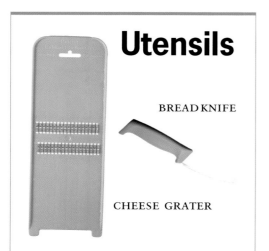

BREAD KNIFE

CHEESE GRATER

4 Place the other slice of bread on top, with the buttered side facing in. Cook the croque-monsieur in a preheated oven at 350 °F (180 °C) for about 15 minutes, turning it over halfway through.

Ham & Cheese Crêpes

(KREP)

Crêpes are one of the most famous of all French dishes, so to be a real French chef, you must learn how to make them. Luckily, they are not very hard to make. Crêpes can be served with salty fillings, such as cheese and ham, or with sweet ones, such as sugar, jam, or chocolate topped with whipped cream. Even today, there are crêpe stands on many street corners in Paris and other cities in France.

TIPS & TRICKS

Each time you add batter to the frying pan, add a little more melted butter first. Hold the pan firmly by the handle as you cook the crêpes. If you do not have Gruyère cheese, use a thin slice of cheddar cheese, or any other cheese that melts well, instead.

Utensils

FRYING PAN

MIXING BOWL

EGG BEATER

WHISK

SLOTTED SPATULA

Ingredients

1 cup (125 g) all-purpose flour

pinch of salt

1 cup (250 ml) milk

2 eggs

2 tablespoons (30 g) butter

8 thin slices Gruyère or other cheese

8 thin slices ham

1 **Sift** the flour and salt into a bowl. Pour in the milk a little at a time, stirring continuously with a whisk or fork.

2 Still stirring with a whisk or egg beater, add the eggs, followed by the melted butter, and stir until the batter is smooth. Place in the fridge for one hour.

3 Melt a little extra butter in a 9-inch (22 cm) frying pan and add a **ladleful** of batter.

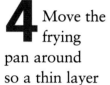

4 Move the frying pan around so a thin layer of batter covers the bottom. Cook until light brown on one side. Use a spatula to flip and cook the other side. Place the crêpe on a plate. Repeat until you have used all the batter.

5 Cover half of each crêpe with a slice of cheese and a slice of ham. Fold the empty half over the top.

6 Return the folded crêpes to the pan long enough to melt the cheese. Serve them warm.

Macaroni with Béchamel *(BAY-shuh-mel)*

Béchamel is a well-known French white sauce. It was invented by Louis de Béchamel, who was head **butler** at the grand court of King Louis XIV in the seventeenth century. Béchamel goes particularly well with pasta but is also delicious with vegetables baked in the oven.

Utensils

CHEESE GRATER

WOODEN SPOON

COLANDER

OVENPROOF BAKING DISH

SAUCEPAN

1 Melt the butter in a saucepan over a low heat. Remove from the heat and sift in the flour, stirring continuously so that no lumps form.

2 Return to the heat and cook for 1 to 2 minutes, so that the flour is lightly browned.

3 Pour in the milk a little at a time, stirring continuously. Add salt, pepper, and nutmeg to taste. After a few minutes, the mixture will boil. Cook for 3 to 4 minutes, stirring all the time.

4 Lightly butter an ovenproof dish and cover the bottom with a layer of cooked macaroni. If you are using long macaroni, curl the pieces around to cover the dish as evenly as you can. You can also use other types of pasta, short or long.

5 Cover the macaroni with a layer of sauce, followed by a layer of Gruyère and a sprinkling of Parmesan. Repeat until all the ingredients are used up.

Ingredients

8 tablespoons (125 g) butter

1 cup (105 g) all-purpose flour

salt and ground black pepper

pinch of freshly grated nutmeg

2 cups (500 ml) milk

10 ounces (300 g) cooked pasta

5 ounces (150 g) Gruyère cheese

2 ounces (60 g) grated Parmesan cheese

TIPS & TRICKS

To cook the macaroni, place a large pan of cold water over a high heat. When it is boiling, add the macaroni and cook for the time indicated on the box. When the macaroni is cooked, ask an adult to help you drain it in the colander.

6 Preheat the oven to 400 °F (200 °C) and bake for about 20 minutes, or until a golden crust, or gratin, has formed. Ask an adult to remove the hot dish and serve straight from the oven.

Tomato Omelette

Omelettes are quick and easy to make. They are also **nutritious** and fun to serve. They can be eaten plain, with herbs, or filled with cheese, tomatoes, ham, or any of your favorite ingredients. Omelettes are also practical. If eggs are the only food you have in your fridge, you can still make this delicious treat.

Ingredients

1 onion

4 ripe tomatoes

2 **tablespoons** olive oil

salt and ground black pepper

6 eggs

1 bunch parsley

1 On a cutting board, slice the onion thinly with a sharp knife. Hold the knife firmly by the handle, and keep your fingers away from the blade. Ask an adult to help.

TIPS & TRICKS

While cooking the omelette, make sure that the handle of the frying pan does not stick out. You might knock it as you pass by and spill it on yourself or the floor.

2 Place a pan of water over high heat. When the water boils, turn off the heat and carefully add the tomatoes. Boil for 2 minutes, then remove with a spoon. When the tomatoes have cooled down, remove the skins with your fingers. Chop the tomatoes into tiny pieces.

3 Heat the oil in a frying pan. Add the onion and tomato, season with salt and pepper, and cook over medium to low heat for 15 minutes. Hold the handle of the pan while you stir it with a wooden spoon.

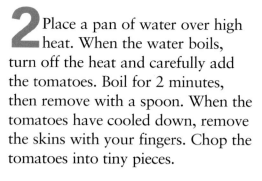

4 Break the eggs into a bowl and beat them quickly with a fork. Season with a little salt.

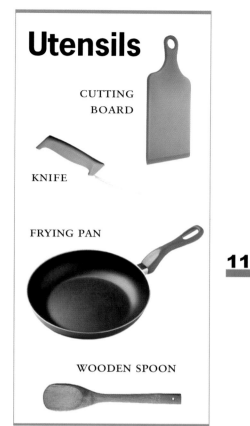

Utensils

CUTTING
BOARD

KNIFE

FRYING PAN

WOODEN SPOON

5 Lightly oil another frying pan and place over medium to low heat. Pour in half the eggs and cook for 4 to 5 minutes. Move the pan gently from side to side as the omelette cooks. Remove the omelette from the heat and slide it onto a serving dish.

6 Cook the second omelette as shown above. Pour half the tomato mixture onto one half of each omelette, sprinkle with chopped parsley, and use a wooden spoon to fold it in two. Serve and enjoy!

11

Quiche Lorraine

(KEESH luh-RAYN)

There are many different types of quiche, but quiche Lorraine is many people's favorite. It was invented by a French cook in the northern city of Nancy in the 16th century. The French serve quiche as a **first course,** but it is so filling that it can be served as a meal by itself.

1 Sift the flour and salt into a mixing bowl. Add the chopped butter and rub it in using your fingers until the mixture is the **consistency** of bread crumbs. Gradually add just enough water to form the mixture into a ball and leave in the fridge for 30 minutes.

Ingredients

3 cups (375 g) all-purpose flour

12 tablespoons (180 g) butter

pinch of salt

dried beans

3 tablespoons ice cold water

4 ounces (125 g) bacon

4 ounces (125 g) Swiss cheese

3 eggs

1 ½ cups (375 ml) cream

pinch of freshly grated nutmeg

TIPS & TRICKS

This quiche is also good if made with ham instead of bacon. Ask an adult to help when putting dishes in or taking them out of the oven and remember to use oven mitts.

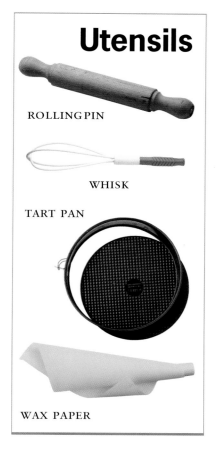

2 Lightly flour a rolling pin and roll the pastry dough out on a floured surface until it is about ¼ inch (5 mm) thick.

3 Use the pastry dough to line a buttered, floured 10-inch (25 cm) tart pan.

4 Prick the pastry dough on the bottom of the dish with a fork. Cover with a sheet of wax paper and fill with the dried beans. Bake in a preheated oven at 400 °F (200 °C) for 20 minutes.

Utensils

ROLLING PIN

WHISK

TART PAN

5 Take the pastry crust out of the oven and throw away the paper and beans. Fry the bacon lightly (you could cut it up into small pieces) and add to the tart pan, with the cheese.

6 Beat the eggs and cream. Add a pinch of salt and nutmeg. Pour the mixture over the bacon and cheese. Bake in a preheated oven at 350 °F (180 °C) for 30 minutes.

WAX PAPER

Salade Niçoise

(sah-LAHD nee-SWAHZ)

This healthy, colorful salad is easy to prepare and requires almost no cooking. Served with freshly baked French bread, it makes a nutritious lunch. Its name comes from Nice, a beautiful city on the Mediterranean Sea, in the south of France. Many fish dishes are served in this region. The ingredients can be changed so that if you do not like onions, for example, you can use another herb or vegetable instead.

1 Wash the vegetables and dry them thoroughly. Slice the red pepper across the middle and remove the seeds and center. Slice it into thin, round strips.

2 Peel and slice the cucumber into thin pieces. Cut the tomatoes into wedges and the onion into thin separated slices. Place the lettuce leaves in a salad bowl.

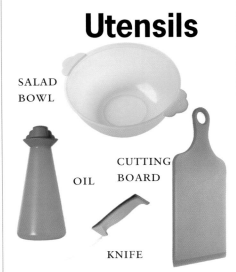

Utensils

SALAD BOWL

OIL

CUTTING BOARD

KNIFE

3 Peel the eggs and cut them in quarters lengthwise. Place the eggs and the other ingredients on top of the lettuce leaves.

4 Sprinkle with a little salt and drizzle with the oil. Use salad servers to toss the ingredients. Try to do this carefully so that the eggs do not fall apart.

TIPS & TRICKS

Be very careful with the knife when you are chopping the vegetables. Ask an adult to help. Hold the knife firmly by the handle and use your other hand to hold the vegetables. Always watch what you are doing, and make sure that your fingertips stay away from the blade of the knife.

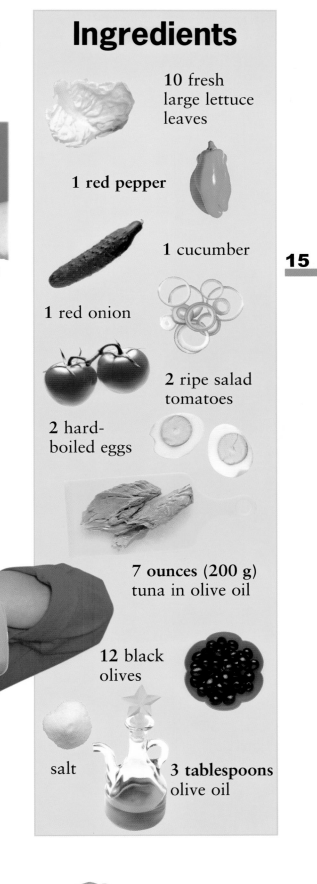

Ingredients

10 fresh large lettuce leaves

1 red pepper

1 cucumber

1 red onion

2 ripe salad tomatoes

2 hard-boiled eggs

7 ounces (200 g) tuna in olive oil

12 black olives

salt

3 tablespoons olive oil

Chicken Skewers

Chicken skewers, or kebabs, are called brochettes in southern France and the Mediterranean island of Corsica. Kebabs are fun to make because you can move around the meat and other ingredients on the skewers to make each one look different. When cooked, you can slide the ingredients off the skewer with a fork. Cherry tomatoes or another vegetable can be used instead of the grapefruit in this recipe.

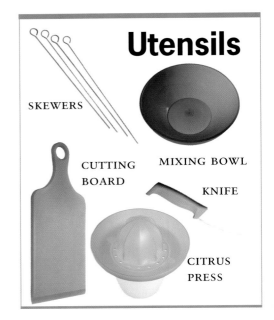

Utensils

SKEWERS

CUTTING BOARD

MIXING BOWL

KNIFE

CITRUS PRESS

1 Place the chicken breasts and pancetta or bacon on a cutting board. Chop them into bite-sized pieces.

2 Cut one of the two grapefruits in half and squeeze out the juice using a citrus press.

3 Beat the grapefruit juice with the olive oil and a little salt and pepper in a bowl. Add the chopped meat and mix well. Set aside to **marinate** for at least 30 minutes. If you have the time, 2 hours is even better.

Ingredients

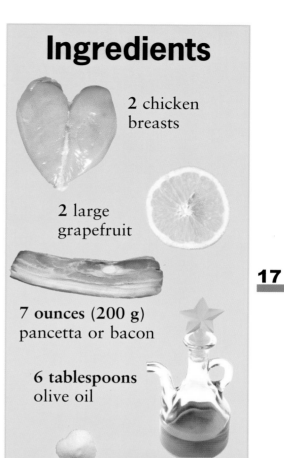

2 chicken breasts

2 large grapefruit

7 **ounces (200 g)** pancetta or bacon

6 **tablespoons** olive oil

salt and freshly ground black pepper

4 Peel the remaining grapefruit, removing as much of the skin and white pith as possible. Ask an adult to help you use a pointed knife to remove the skin covering each wedge.

TIPS & TRICKS

If using wooden skewers, soak them well in cold water first so they do not burn. These kebabs can be cooked over a barbecue or in the oven.

5 Stick a piece of chicken onto a skewer, then follow with a piece of pancetta, and then a piece of grapefruit. Repeat until the skewer is full. When all the kebabs are ready, grill them for about 15 minutes. Turn them often during cooking and sprinkle with a little salt. Ask an adult to help you.

La Fête des Rois
(LAH FET DAY RWAH)

La Fête des Rois, the Feast of the Kings, takes place in France on Epiphany, celebrated on January 6. Epiphany is an ancient Christian festival in memory of the three kings (the three wise men) who went to Bethlehem to worship Jesus soon after he was born. In France, a special *galette,* or cake, is baked with a *fève,* or bean, hidden inside. Whoever finds the bean in his piece of cake is king for a day. Invite your friends to a party. Bake the galette and put a secret mark on top where the bean is located that only you will recognize. Since you are the host, do not take that piece. The youngest guest hides under the table and calls the name of the next person to receive a slice of cake.

Remember to put the bean in the cake mixture.

La Galette des Rois

- **8 tablespoons (125 g)** butter
- **1 cup (125 g)** sugar
- **3 eggs**
- **1 cup (125 g)** finely ground almonds
- **2 round pieces of puff pastry, 12 inches (30 cm)** in diameter

Beat the butter and sugar until creamy. Stir in two eggs, then add the almonds. Line a greased cake pan with one of the pieces of pastry. Fill with the almond mixture. Beat the remaining egg and brush it over the edges of the pastry. Place the other piece of pastry on top and seal well. Use a knife to make patterns in the pastry. Brush the rest of the beaten egg over the top. Bake in a preheated oven at 400 °F (200 °C) for 30 minutes. Serve warm.

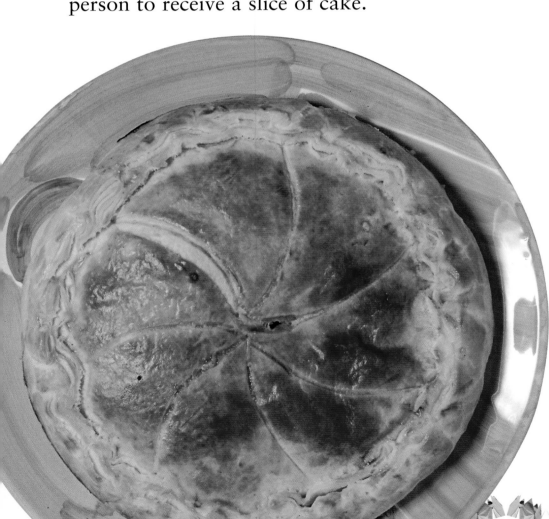

This painting is by the Italian artist Gentile da Fabriano. He painted it in 1423. It shows the three kings worshipping the baby Jesus. The kings traveled from the East to Bethlehem. They followed a bright star.

Buy some colored paper and prepare crowns for your guests to wear. Make one extra special crown for the person who finds the bean in her piece of cake.

Ground Beef & Potato Pie

In France, this dish is called *hachis Parmentier*. The combination of ground meat and potato purée tastes so good that this may become one of your favorite French dishes. Potatoes were not always popular in France. When Antoine-Augustin Parmentier (after whom the dish was named) began growing potatoes around 1785, no one liked them. Parmentier had to use tricks just to get people to taste them!

Utensils

POTATO PEELER

CHOPPER

MASHER

MIXING SPOON

FRYING PAN

OVENPROOF BAKING DISH

1 Peel the potatoes and cook them in boiling water for about 20 minutes, or until a fork slides into one easily. Drain the water and place the potatoes in a bowl.

2 Mash the potatoes with a potato masher. Add half the butter and keep mashing. Gradually add the milk to make a smooth, creamy mixture. Season with salt and nutmeg.

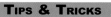

TIPS & TRICKS

Remember to turn the oven on about 15 minutes before you finish preparing the pie so that it will be hot when you are ready to cook. Always ask an adult for help when using the oven.

Ingredients

2 pounds (1 kg) potatoes

2 cups (500 ml) milk

6 tablespoons (90 g) butter

10 ounces (300 g) cooked meat or raw ground beef

1 large onion

bunch of parsley

salt

pinch of freshly grated nutmeg

3 If you are using cooked meat, chop or mince the meat until it is in small pieces. Chop the onion and cut the parsley into fine bits.

4 Melt half the remaining butter in a pan and fry the onion and parsley. Add the meat and season with salt. Cook for 5 minutes over a medium heat for cooked meat, or 15 minutes if you are using raw meat.

5 Grease the ovenproof dish with a little butter and cover with a layer of potato. Sprinkle with the parsley, then add the meat. Cover with the remaining potato and top with the butter.

6 Bake in a preheated oven at 400 °F (200 °C) for 20 minutes.

Sole Meunière
(SOHL muh-NYER)

Sole is such a tasty fish that the ancient Romans called the fish *solea jovis*, or Jupiter's sandal, in honor of one of their gods. Chefs have found many different ways of serving it in French cuisine. This recipe is called *sole meunière,* or miller's sole. The fish is dipped in flour and **sautéed** in butter to make a tasty sauce.

TIPS & TRICKS

Turning the fish in the pan is tricky. Ask an adult to help you with this step. Make sure you remove the pan from the heat while you do it. Any kind of small thin fish or fish filet can be used for this recipe.

Sprinkle the fish with parsley before serving. Serve it hot!

1 Place the flour in a large flat-bottomed bowl or plate. Dip each fish in the flour, making sure it is well coated on both sides.

Depending on the size of your pan, add half of the butter for two fish or a quarter if only one fish will fit.

2 Melt the butter in a nonstick pan over low heat. Add a drop of oil to the pan to prevent the butter from burning.

Ingredients

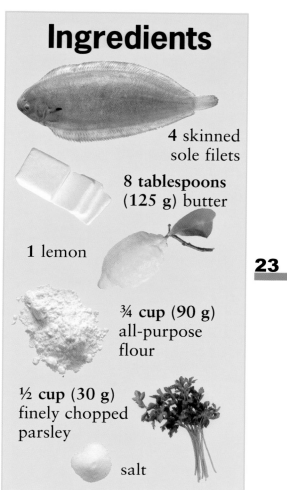

4 skinned sole filets

8 tablespoons (125 g) butter

1 lemon

¾ cup (90 g) all-purpose flour

½ cup (30 g) finely chopped parsley

salt

3 Add the fish to the pan and cook over low heat. After about 5 minutes, flip the fish with a slotted spatula. Cook for another 5 minutes. Season with salt.

4 While the fish is cooking, squeeze the juice from the lemon.

5 When the fish is almost cooked, pour half the lemon juice over the fish and cook for 1 more minute. Slip the fish in the pan onto a serving dish and cook the rest.

Utensils

FRYING PAN

SLOTTED SPATULA

CITRUS PRESS

Strawberry Tart

France is the third-largest producer of strawberries in the world. It is not surprising, then, that the French were the inventors of this delicious tart. Strawberries are grown in the Rhone valley, Brittany, and other areas of France. They are full of vitamins and are very good for you.

1 Put the flour in a bowl. Add the butter and rub it in with your fingers until the mixture has the consistency of bread crumbs. Stir in the **separated** egg yolks, then roll the dough together into a ball. Wrap it in plastic wrap and place in the fridge for about 30 minutes.

2 Sprinkle some flour on a rolling pin and roll out the dough on a floured surface until it is about ¼ inch (5mm) thick.

3 Use the dough to line a buttered and floured 10-inch (26 cm) in diameter loose-bottomed tart pan. Cover with a sheet of wax paper and fill with dried beans. Bake in a preheated oven at 350 °F (180 °C) for about 20 minutes.

4 Remove the crust from the oven and throw out the paper and beans. Arrange the strawberries, pointed end facing up, on the pastry crust.

Utensils

WAX PAPER

MIXING BOWL

ROLLING PIN

PASTRY BRUSH

TART PAN WITH LOOSE BOTTOM

5 **Dilute** the jam with 2–3 tablespoons of warm water. Use a new, clean pastry brush to paint the tops of the strawberries with the jam. Remove from the dish and serve at room temperature with ice cream or whipped cream.

Ingredients

2 cups (250 g) all-purpose flour

8 tablespoons (125 g) butter

2 egg yolks

½ cup (200 g) strawberry jam

2 pounds (1 kg) clean, fresh strawberries

dried beans

TIPS & TRICKS

Ask an adult to help you separate the egg yolks from the egg whites. If strawberries are out of season, use the same quantity of raspberries and raspberry jam instead.

Chocolate Mousse

Soft, fluffy, and sweet, mousse is almost pure chocolate and will be a favorite with your family and friends. Chocolate mousse is one of the easiest French desserts to make. It became a popular treat in the 1970s with the introduction of **nouvelle cuisine**. The best part about preparing this recipe is cleaning up and licking the spoons!

1 Put the chocolate in a small saucepan with the milk and then put the saucepan into a larger pan of cold water. Place over medium heat, and stir until the chocolate melts.

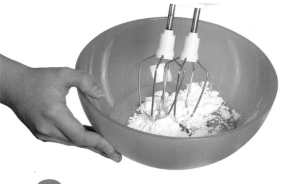

2 In a bowl, beat the separated egg yolks with the sugar until they are pale and creamy. Stir it into the melted chocolate.

Utensils

SPATULA

ELECTRIC MIXER

SMALL SAUCEPAN

SAUCEPAN

3 Beat the egg whites with a pinch of salt until they form stiff peaks. **Fold** the beaten egg whites into the chocolate, taking care that the egg whites do not lose their stiffness.

4 Beat the cream with an electric mixer or whisk until thick. Fold it carefully into the chocolate and egg mixture.

Ingredients

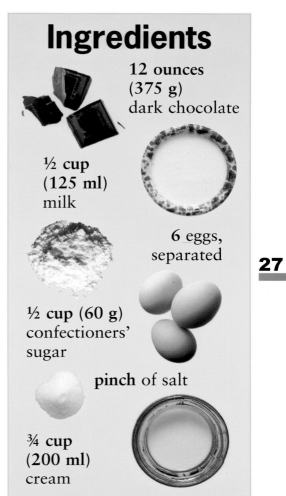

12 ounces (375 g) dark chocolate

½ cup (125 ml) milk

6 eggs, separated

½ cup (60 g) confectioners' sugar

pinch of salt

¾ cup (200 ml) cream

27

TIPS & TRICKS

Be careful when melting the chocolate. Ask an adult to help you separate the egg yolks from the whites. Do not overwhip the cream in step 4, or it will turn into butter.

5 Put the mousse mixture into individual dessert dishes or one large serving bowl. Leave in the fridge for at least 4 hours before serving. Add whipped cream if desired.

Profiteroles

(*pruh-FEE-teh-rohl*)

You may have seen this delicious-looking dessert in the window of a bakery. Now you can make it at home. To make things easier, you can buy the pastry cases ready-made. Then just fill them with ice cream, dip them in chocolate, and decorate with whipped cream.

28

Ingredients

7 ounces (200 g) dark chocolate

10 ounces (300 g) ready-made choux pastry cases

10 ounces (300 g) vanilla ice cream

1 cup (250 ml) whipping cream

1 Carefully use a knife to break up the chocolate. Put it into a small saucepan and then put the pan into a larger pan of cold water. Place the saucepan over medium heat and melt the chocolate.

TIPS & TRICKS

Take the ice cream out of the freezer just before you begin to fill the profiteroles. If you take it out too early, it will melt while you work. You can also try filling the profiteroles with vanilla custard or whipped cream instead of ice cream. You could add some fruit sauce on top of everything.

2 Make a small hole in each pastry case. Using a pastry chef's syringe, fill each one with ice cream.

3 Arrange the filled profiteroles one on top of the other in a pyramid shape. Use a little of the melted chocolate to stick them together.

4 Pour the remaining chocolate over the top so that it runs down the sides. Beat the cream until it is thick. Fill the syringe with the whipped cream and decorate the stack of profiteroles.

Utensils

ELECTRIC MIXER

KNIFE

PASTRY CHEF'S SYRINGE

SPATULA

Crème Brûlée

(KREM broo-LAY)

Crème brûlée means "burned custard" in French, but this dessert is not actually burned. When broiled, the brown sugar on the top forms a melt-in-the-mouth crust, which combines well with the creamy vanilla custard underneath. To really enjoy crème brûlée, serve it while it is still a little warm.

Ingredients

7 egg yolks

⅔ cup (150 g) sugar

2 cups (500 ml) cream

½ cup (100 ml) milk

⅓ cup (60 g) brown sugar

1 Ask an adult to separate the egg yolks from the whites. Then, in a bowl, beat the egg yolks with the sugar until it is pale and creamy.

TIPS & TRICKS

Ask an adult to help you place the pan in the oven. You must be careful not to spill water in the oven. When checking to see if the crème brûlée is cooked, and when broiling the sugar, remember to wear thick oven mitts.

2 Heat the cream and milk together. Just before they boil, remove from the heat and pour them into the egg and sugar mixture, beating continuously.

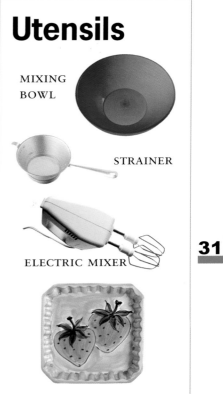

Utensils

MIXING BOWL

STRAINER

ELECTRIC MIXER

BAKING DISH

3 Filter the mixture using a strainer.

4 Pour the mixture into a buttered ovenproof dish. Put the dish in a larger dish or pan, such as a roasting pan, filled with cold water. Place both dishes in a preheated oven at 350 °F (180 °C), and cook for 1 hour. Ask an adult to help you with this. When a toothpick comes out clean, the crème brûlée is ready.

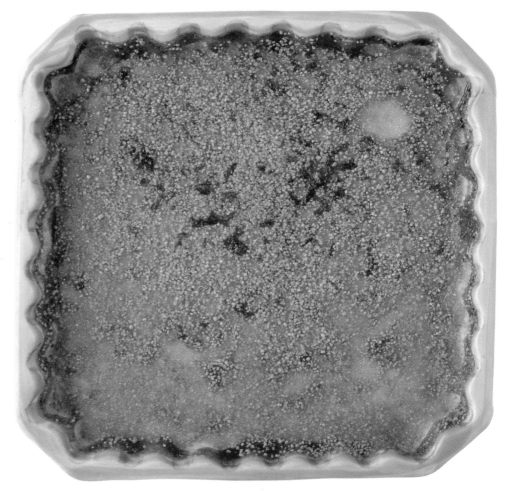

5 Remove from the oven and set aside to cool. Sprinkle with the brown sugar and place under the broiler for 5 minutes until the sugar is brown and crisp.

Glossary

butler (BUT-ler) The head male servant of a household, in charge of the other servants and serving meals.

consistency (kun-SIS-tent-see) The firmness of a mixture.

cuisine (kwih-ZEEN) A style or way of cooking food.

dilute (dy-LOOT) To make a liquid thinner by adding water.

first course (FURST KAWRS) The first part of a dinner.

fold (FOHLD) To add another ingredient to a mixture by gently turning one part over another.

Gruyère (groo-YER) A pale yellow Swiss cheese.

ladleful (LAY-dul-ful) The amount of liquid that fills a ladle, a kitchen tool with a cup-shaped bowl.

marinate (MER-uh-nayt) To let food sit in a liquid mixture, usually of vinegar or wine, oil, herbs, and spices, for a period of time before cooking.

nouvelle cuisine (noo-vel kwih-ZEEN) A style of cooking using fresh ingredients, a variety of foods, and light sauces served in a decorative way.

nutritious (noo-TRIH-shus) Healthy to eat.

sautéed (saw-TAYD) Cooked or browned in a pan with a small quantity of butter or oil.

separated (SEH-puh-rayt-ed) Divided an egg's yolk from its white.

sift (SIFT) To separate out any coarse grains of flour so only fine flour is used.

sprinkle (SPRING-kul) To scatter around.

trim (TRIM) To remove the extra or unwanted parts of a piece of food.

Index

Web Sites

Due to the changing nature of Internet links, PowerKids Press has developed an online list of Web sites related to the subject of this book. This site is updated regularly. Please use this link to access the list: www.powerkidslinks.com/lgc/french/